Beginner Biography

Sojourner Truth

Fighting for Freedom

by Jeri Cipriano
illustrated by Scott R. Brooks

LOOK!
BOOKS™

Red Chair Press   Egremont, Massachusetts

Look! Books are produced and published by Red Chair Press:

Red Chair Press LLC   PO Box 333   South Egremont, MA 01258-0333

www.redchairpress.com

 FREE lesson guide at www.redchairpress.com/free-activities

Publisher's Cataloging-In-Publication Data

Names: Cipriano, Jeri S., author. | Brooks, Scott R., 1963- illustrator.

Title: Sojourner Truth: fighting for freedom / by Jeri Cipriano;
illustrated by Scott R. Brooks.

Description: Egremont, Massachusetts : Red Chair Press, [2020] | Series:
Look! books. Beginner biography | Includes index and resources for
further reading. | Interest age level: 005-008. | Summary: "Sojourner
Truth was born to slaves. She had no choice. But when she grew to be a
young mother herself, she ran away with her child looking for freedom.
She used her voice to speak for all slaves wanting to be free."-- Provided by publisher.

Identifiers: ISBN 9781634409933 (library hardcover) | ISBN 9781634409940
(paperback) | ISBN 9781634409957 (ebook)

Subjects: LCSH: Truth, Sojourner, 1799-1883--Juvenile literature. |
African American women abolitionists--Biography--Juvenile literature. |
African American women--Biography--Juvenile literature. | Slavery--
United States--History--19th century--Juvenile literature. | CYAC:
Truth, Sojourner, 1799-1883. | African American women abolitionists--
Biography. | African American women--Biography. | Slavery--United
States--History--19th century.

Classification: LCC E185.97.T8 C35 2020 (print) | E185.97.T8 (ebook) | DDC
305.5/67/092 B--dc23

Library of Congress Control Number: 2019938781

Photo credits: p. 4: Library of Congress; p. 14: Courtesy of Paul Hernandez/Special
Collections, F.W. Olin Library, Mills College; p. 20: Associated Press

Printed in the United States of America

0819 1P CGS20

Table of Contents

A Name to Remember

Your name is important. It tells who you are and which family you belong to.

Years ago, one strong woman gave herself a new name when she was no longer a **slave**.
This is her story.

I Sell the Shadow to Support the Substance.
SOJOURNER TRUTH.

Baby Belle

In 1797, a baby girl was born to two slaves on a farm in New York State. They named her Isabella and called her *Belle* for short.

Belle was sold for $100. Her owner added a flock of sheep to sell her more quickly.

Slaves belonged to their owners, not to each other. When Belle was 9, she and her brother were sold to different families.

Life as a Slave

Belle worked hard. She grew tall and strong like her father. When it was time to marry, her owner picked a husband for her. He promised them **freedom** after ten years.

Ten years passed, but nothing changed. So, in 1826, Belle ran away, taking her baby, Sophia, with her.

Good to Know

It was against the law to sell slaves outside of New York. Belle went to **court** and got her son back. Imagine that! A former slave winning in court.

Freedom!

Some people were against slavery. These people helped slaves who were running away. Belle soon moved in with a **Quaker** family.

In 1827, New York freed all its slaves. Belle was free! But she had to save her son, Peter. He had been sold to someone in Alabama.

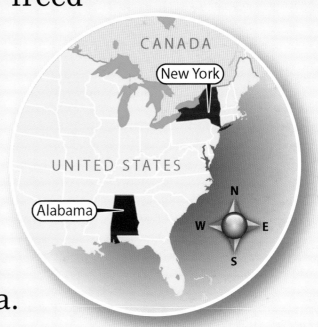

New Life, New Name

Belle moved to New York City when she was about 30 years old. She worked cleaning people's homes. She joined a church and started speaking out against slavery.

In 1843, Belle took the name *Sojourner Truth*. She traveled from place to place telling the truth about slavery and how **cruel** it was.

Good to Know

Sojourner means someone who
stays only a short time in a place.

The Story of Her Life

Sojourner told the story of her life to a friend who turned it into a book. Sojourner then sold her book to crowds that gathered to hear her speak.

Good to Know

Sojourner never learned how to read or write, but her speeches gave people hope.

Women's Rights

At the time, women did not have the same **rights** as men, so Sojourner started speaking for women's rights, too.

Good to Know

Sojourner stood six feet tall. She was strong and could work as hard as any man. She used this fact in her speeches.

A Life of Service

Sojourner was close to 70 years old in 1865 when a change to the Constitution ended slavery in the United States.

When she died in 1883 in Michigan, more than 1,000 people came to her funeral.

Good to Know

On Dec 18, 1865 the 13th Amendment to the U.S. Constitution was officially approved ending slavery.

President Abraham Lincoln signed Sojourner's book. He thanked her for her work for freedoms.

19

Sojourner Truth worked to end slavery and to get equal rights for women. She believed all people should be equal and free.

In 1997, the U.S. sent a space machine all the way to the planet Mars. It was named Sojourner in honor of Sojourner Truth.

Timeline: Big Dates in Sojourner's Life

1797: Isabella is born a slave in New York State.

1806: Belle is sold at age nine.

1815: Belle marries Thomas, also a slave.

1826: Belle runs away with her daughter Sophia.

1827: New York State frees its slaves.

1828: Belle wins court case to get her son back.

1829: Moves to New York with her son Peter.

1843: She names herself *Sojourner Truth*.

1851: Sojourner makes a big speech in Ohio for Women's Rights.

1857: She moves to Michigan.

1861: The **Civil War** begins.

1865: The Civil War ends, and so does slavery.

1883: Sojourner Truth dies on November 26.

In 1986, the Post Office made a stamp to honor Sojourner Truth.

Words to Know

Civil War the U.S. war that was fought between northern states and southern states

court a place where legal cases are heard and decided

cruel causing pain to others

freedom the right to do and say what you like

Quaker member of the Society of Friends, a group opposed to slavery

rights what you have or can do under the law

slave a person who is owned by another person and is forced to work

Learn More at the Library

(Check out these books to read with others)

Adler, David. *A Picture Book of Sojourner Truth.* Holiday House, 1994.

Merchant, Peter. *Sojourner Truth: Path to Glory (ready to Read).* Simon Spotlight, 2007.

McDonough, Yona Zeldis. *Who Was Sojourner Truth?* Penguin Young Readers, 2015.

Turner, Ann. *A My Name is Truth: The Life of Sojourner Truth.* Harper Collins, 2015.

Index

About the Author

Jeri Cipriano has written more than a hundred books for young readers. She enjoys reading and finding out new things. She likes to share what she learns.